Original title:
The Seal's Smile

Copyright © 2024 Swan Charm
All rights reserved.

Editor: Jessica Elisabeth Luik
Author: Olivia Orav
ISBN HARDBACK: 978-9916-86-413-5
ISBN PAPERBACK: 978-9916-86-414-2

Tidal Amusement

Waves of laughter dance on the shore
Salty breeze feels like before.
Sandcastles stand, then fade away,
Whispers of the sea, in play.

Footprints trace our joyful chase,
Nature's rhythm, a lively pace.
Shells collect tales from afar,
Beneath the moon, a guiding star.

Oceans sing to hearts untamed,
Children play, unbowed, unnamed.
In tidal pools, life's hidden gems,
Reflect the world's vibrant diadems.

Hands held tight, we share a smile,
Bound by the sea, mile by mile.
In every wave, an endless song,
Tidal amusement, pure and strong.

Day by day, the tides repeat,
A symphony of joy replete.
Memories carved in coastal sand,
Eternal fun on ocean's strand.

Wet Whispers

Wet whispers glide on evening's breath,
Secrets shared in water's depth.
A symphony in gentle hum,
Where silence merges, becomes one.

Rippled murmurs, soft and clear,
Drawing close, yet nowhere near.
Echoes of the ocean's past,
In currents strong, their truths are cast.

Mysteries fold in endless night,
Darkened waves by moonlight bright.
Whispers carried, wide and far,
Wet confessions, what we are.

Rippling Joy

Sunlight dancing on the stream,
A golden thread, a waking dream.
Leaves whisper secrets, oh so coy,
In the current, rippling joy.

Nature's laughter, skies that beam,
Joyful ripples, a tranquil theme.
Pebbles whisper, songs employ,
In the flow, pure rippling joy.

Sea Mist Grin

The sea mist forms a gentle grin,
As waves crash loud, yet peace within.
A dance of light on waters sheer,
Salt-kissed air, voices clear.

Morning breaks with hues of blue,
Secrets whispered, always true.
Sailors' tales of love and loss,
In misty wraps, their paths they cross.

Windswept hair, a siren's call,
Echoes, drift where shadows fall.
Sand beneath and skies so vast,
The sea mist grins, our stories cast.

Ebb and Flow

Moonlit tides, a silver show,
Mystic rhythms, ebb and flow.
Waves embrace the sandy shore,
In their dance, forevermore.

Whispers of the ocean's woe,
Silent echoes come and go.
Nature's pulse, both high and low,
In the heart, the ebb and flow.

Sunlit Waters

Sunlit waters, crystal gleam,
Reflecting dreams, a sunbeam's dream.
Under skies where bluebirds soar,
We find a peace, forevermore.

Waves that kiss the golden shore,
Whispers soft, forevermore.
In the light of day's embrace,
We find our hearts, an open space.

Sailing on where skies abide,
With the sun, our spirits glide.
In sunlit waters, pure and free,
We find the essence of the sea.

Currents of Joy

Beneath the waves where sunlight plays,
A dance of light in watery maze.
Fish dart by in carefree swirls,
Their hues like gems, their forms like pearls.

Seaweed sways in the gentle tide,
Embracing the ocean, arms open wide.
Currents flow with secrets untold,
Whispers of joy in the deep blue cold.

A dolphin leaps, a joyous arc,
Splashing down with a playful spark.
In this realm of endless blue,
Happiness swims, forever true.

Nautical Happiness

Sails unfurl, the winds do sing,
Nautical dreams on seagulls' wing.
Horizons kiss where waters twine,
In the wake, so clear and fine.

Journeys start as anchors spring,
Happiness in waves we bring.
Compass points to stars that shine,
In the sea's embrace, divine.

Smirking Waves

Playful foam on sandy shore,
Smirking waves with tales of lore.
Breathing life in bubbly staves,
Chuckle softly, smirking waves.

Sun is setting, day withdraws,
Waves still laugh with little cause.
Endless whispers, ocean's braves,
In their curl, the smirking waves.

Tidal Tune

A melody of ebb and flow,
Tides that sing the moonlight's glow.
In rhythm, hearts both fast and slow,
The tidal tune that we all know.

Stars above and waves below,
In this harmony, we grow.
Whispers soft and currents strong,
A timeless symphony life long.

Ocean's breath and sailor's song,
In this dance, we all belong.
Through tempest high and calm so low,
The song of tides, forever flow.

Splash of Laughter

Laughter echoes through the bay,
Children's joy in sunlight's ray.
Waves come crashing, wild and free,
Mingling with shouts of glee.

Sandcastles rise from grains of dreams,
Mystical forts where sunlight gleams.
Tiny hands build towers high,
Reaching towards the endless sky.

Seagulls caw in high delight,
Joining in the children's light.
In the splash and in the cheer,
Laughter flows, so pure, so clear.

Aquatic Whisper

Moonlight casts a silver sheen,
Over waters calm, serene.
Soft whispers of the ocean's song,
Sing to those who drift along.

Stars reflect in rippled sleep,
Secrets in the waters deep.
A gentle breeze stirs the night,
Carrying whispers of the light.

In the quiet, where dreams unfurl,
The aquatic whisper calms the world.
In harmony with the night's embrace,
The ocean whispers its own grace.

Glimmering Beneath

Beneath the surface, hidden gold,
Stories of the deep untold.
Glimmers of light in watery dark,
Each a memory, each a spark.

Coral reefs with vibrant hues,
Guard these tales and ancient clues.
Creatures glide in silent grace,
In this secret, precious space.

With every stroke, with every dive,
The depths come alive.
Glimmering beneath, a world unseen,
A liquid realm, serene, pristine.

Saltwater Dance

Beneath the moon's soft glowing trance,
Each wave performs its saltwater dance.
Oceans whisper secrets in the night,
A liquid ballet under silver light.

Stars align in the sky's vast expanse,
Reflected in the sea's timeless prance.
Seagulls call in a distant romance,
Joining the waves in a fateful chance.

Underneath the swells and spray,
Ocean currents find their way.
Echoes of the deep, a resonant hum,
Nature's song on a timeless drum.

Gentle Waves

Gentle waves kiss the sandy shore,
Quiet ripples whisper more.
The lullaby of the ocean's lore,
Nature's calm, an endless score.

Foam dances lightly on the crest,
In a soothing rhythmic quest.
Ebb and flow, a constant guest,
Earth's pulse put to the test.

In moonlight's tender, soft embrace,
Water shimmers with tranquil grace.
An orchestra of peace and space,
A gentle wave in the quiet race.

Playful Waters

Playful waters splash and glide,
In the oceans, joy resides.
Dolphins leap and currents slide,
In this vast aquatic ride.

Sunlight sparkles on the sea,
Nature's playground, wild and free.
Beneath the waves, a symphony,
Of life's eternal jubilee.

Tides embrace and then release,
In this dance of endless peace.
Water spins and does not cease,
In its playful, flowing crease.

Marine Melody

A marine melody in the deep,
Where ancient secrets gently sleep.
Waves compose a sound so sweet,
Nature's pulse, a rhythmic beat.

Coral reefs hold colors bright,
In underwater's mystic light.
Each creature joins the soft delight,
In the ocean's silent night.

Currents sway in charming grace,
Moving in time and keeping pace.
Water sings in every place,
A marine melody we embrace.

Beneath the Surface

In depths where light does rarely tread,
A world unseen, a life unsaid.
Creatures drift in shadows deep,
Secrets in the water keep.

Coral gardens, colors bright,
In the darkness, there's their light.
Silent songs and whispers blend,
In this realm, time has no end.

Echoes of the past confined,
In currents strong, in ties that bind.
Mysteries of ancient lore,
Lie in wait on ocean floor.

Hidden gems, both rough and rare,
Await the ones who truly dare.
Dive beyond the surface sheen,
And uncover what's unseen.

Ocean's Embrace

Waves that call with gentle ease,
Whispers from the deepest seas.
Horizon meets the sky with grace,
In the ocean's vast embrace.

Foamy crests that kiss the shore,
Endless cycles, evermore.
In the cradle of the blue,
Dreams are born, and hopes renew.

Dolphins dance in liquid gold,
Stories of the sea unfold.
Harmony in every wave,
Life's secrets the waters save.

Underneath the moon's soft glow,
Tides of wonder ebb and flow.
In the swell of ocean's arms,
Find solace in its calming charms.

Dancing Tides

Moonlight calls the ocean's song,
Rhythms ancient, voices strong.
Tides that waltz to lunar tune,
Underneath the silver moon.

Ripples in a dance so fine,
Weaving patterns, intertwine.
In the play of light and shade,
Stories of the sea are made.

Waves that crash with joyous might,
Celebration in the night.
In the depths, a ballet pure,
Nature's dance forever sure.

Ebb and flow, a ceaseless beat,
Motions grand, a cosmic feat.
In the heart of ocean's tides,
Lie the dreams the sea confides.

Underwater Harmony

Beneath the waves so calm and still,
Lies a world of sheer goodwill.
In the silent, azure deep,
Life's secrets in rhythm sleep.

Fish in schools like dancers glide,
Harmony on every side.
Anemones in colors bright,
Wave in currents, pure delight.

Whales with songs that echo far,
Voyage 'neath the ocean bar.
In their notes, the tales of old,
Stories of the deep are told.

Seaweed sways in symphony,
Bound in underwater glee.
In this world of fluid grace,
Find a perfect, peaceful space.

Surf's Delight

Waves rush to greet the shore's embrace,
Golden beams in morning's grace.
Foam-kissed sands with dreams alight,
Endless dance in surf's delight.

Board and rider skim the waves,
Joyous echoes, ocean's praise.
Salt and breeze in sweet caress,
Nature's song in fluid dress.

Amber eve, a painted sky,
Seagulls call, they swoop and fly.
Twilight shadows gently creep,
In surf's arms, the world asleep.

Undersea Gleam

Coral kingdoms bathed in blue,
Fish in hues of vibrant hue.
Ebb and flow through secret seams,
Come and see the undersea gleam.

Jellyfish, they softly pulse,
Glowing lights, a silent waltz.
Mystic caves and sunken beams,
Guardians of ancient dreams.

Glimmered scales and whispered songs,
Mermaids dance where time belongs.
Eternal calm in these streams,
Life abounds where beauty teems.

Tidal Merriment

Tides retreat and tides return,
Whispers of the ocean churn.
Children laugh and seagulls cry,
Beneath the open, azure sky.

Sand castles rise, then fall with glee,
Transient homes to shell and sea.
Footprints kiss the slick, wet shore,
Ebb and flow forevermore.

Kites ascend on salted air,
Dreams take flight with little care.
Hearts are light, as waves are sent,
In the joy of tidal merriment.

Marine Mirth

Glistening surf on pebbled ground,
Echoes of a joyous sound.
Dolphins leap in ocean's mirth,
Celebrating life's rebirth.

Children's laughter intertwines,
Lapping waves in playful lines.
Sun-splashed water, heavens girth,
Inhale the bliss of marine mirth.

Sailboats drift with gentle sway,
In the cradle of the bay.
Nature's chorus, hearts uplift,
With each tide, a sacred gift.

Waves of Joy

Upon the shore where dreams take flight,
The waves of joy dance in the light.
Children laugh, their spirits high,
Underneath the azure sky.

Foam kisses sand with tender grace,
In this sacred, blissful place.
Nature's symphony plays along,
As hearts unite in cheerful song.

Seagulls soar with freedom's might,
Their calls dissolve in morning light.
The ocean whispers secrets old,
Stories of joy, forever told.

Harbor Hilarity

Boats bobbing in an endless play,
In the harbor where mirth holds sway.
Laughter echoes from ship to shore,
Filling hearts forevermore.

Fishermen's tales weave through the air,
Colored with joy, devoid of care.
Sunlight dances on waves so free,
Reflecting glee for all to see.

The anchor drops and with a cheer,
Another day of fun appears.
In the harbor, jokes abound,
Where endless smiles can be found.

Submerged Laughter

Beneath the waves where sunlight dips,
Submerged laughter lightly skips.
Fish in play, a joyous crew,
In waters deep, a world anew.

Coral castles, bright and fair,
Echo laughs that fill the air.
Dolphins leap in gleeful chase,
In this secret, happy place.

Anemones sway with blissful jest,
A whimsical undersea fest.
Submerged in joy, all fears erased,
In the ocean's warm embrace.

Liquid Gold

Golden rays on water spread,
Liquid gold where hopes are fed.
Sunset's brush paints twilight skies,
As day bids gentle, soft goodbyes.

Reflections gleam with stories old,
Tales of joy in liquid gold.
Waves adorned in twilight's light,
Embrace the coming of the night.

In this sea of golden hue,
Dreams and wonders all renew.
As the evening stars unfold,
Hearts are warmed by liquid gold.

Briny Laughter

Waves crash with playful glee,
Their echoes fill the sand.
Children dance, forever free,
In this sea-kissed wonderland.

Foam-tipped giggles, salty spray,
Nature's joyful burst.
Seagulls join in by the bay,
Their songs quench a sailor's thirst.

Pebbles tell their ancient tales,
As tides sweep them anew.
Each shell and stone, the wind exhales,
A chorus for the view.

Sun sets on the horizon's beam,
Gold spills in liquid cheer.
In briny dreams, the sea's esteem,
Dissolves our every fear.

Deep Blue Bliss

Oceans wide, a boundless stretch,
Deep blue hues entrancing.
Currents weave a mystic sketch,
In waves forever dancing.

Sunlight pierces through the crest,
Illuminates the soul.
Whales sing from their hidden nest,
In a world profound and whole.

Beneath the surface, life abounds,
In a silent, fluid chant.
Each creature in its sphere resounds,
A harmony so grand.

Moonlight shimmer, calm descends,
On waters vast and wide.
In deep blue bliss our spirits blend,
With every rolling tide.

Aquatic Symphony

Dolphins leap in arcs so grand,
Joyful notes they bring.
Orchestras of waves and sand,
In ocean's vastest ring.

Coral reefs, with colors bright,
Compose a radiant score.
Fish like notes in rainbow light,
Dance forevermore.

Sirens sing through waters clear,
Their melodies entice.
Every splash, a voice we hear,
In realms beyond our sights.

Tempests rise with thunder's might,
A symphonic, wild embrace.
Calm returns by morning light,
In this eternal space.

Seafloor Serenade

Deep beneath where sunlight fades,
A world of dreams takes hold.
In the seafloor's whispered glades,
Tales and secrets old.

Anemones in gentle sways,
Perform their silent dance.
Quiet tunes in hidden bays,
Where mysteries enhance.

Crabs and lobsters move in time,
To nature's soft refrain.
Their rhythms mark the ocean's chime,
A harmony to sustain.

Midnight hues, a velvet sheet,
Embrace the tranquil view.
In this serenade, life beats,
In deep and endless blue.

Reflection of Joy

In a mirror's quiet gleam,
Where sunlight starts to play,
A whispering dream,
Awakes a golden day.

Petals kissed by morning's dew,
Serenades the butterflies in flight,
Echoes of joy in colors new,
Painting smiles with light.

Laughter dances on the breeze,
Tickling leaves with gentle cheer,
In this peace, the heart finds ease,
Every worry disappears.

Each moment dressed in bliss,
Time's gentle, fleeting ploy,
In simple things, the silent kiss,
The reflection of pure joy.

Marine Whispers

Waves sing ballads to the shore,
Soft and ancient, clear and true,
Salt-kissed breezes evermore,
Bring the sea's secrets anew.

Dolphins play in sapphire dance,
Curving arcs of liquid grace,
In the ocean's deep expanse,
Life reveals its hidden face.

Shells whisper tales to the sand,
Mysteries of the deep,
Each one a treasure, finely tanned,
In the silence, secrets keep.

Stars reflected in the tide,
Glimmering paths in night's embrace,
In marine whispers, we confide,
The ocean's calm and gentle pace.

Ocean's Embrace

Beneath the azure, waves arise,
A waltz with time, in liquid grace,
Sunset mirrored in the skies,
In the ocean's warm embrace.

Seagulls call from distant ships,
Echoes of the voyage they trace,
Each horizon, kissed by lips,
Of the boundless sea's embrace.

Coral gardens paint the deep,
With colors vivid, spaces wide,
Hidden realms where secrets sleep,
Beneath the ocean's gentle tide.

Tides that ebb and flow with time,
Whispering tales of love and space,
In each heartbeat, so sublime,
We find the ocean's true embrace.

Whispers of Cheer

Morning light, a golden thread,
Weaves through dreams, so soft, so near,
Chasing shadows from our head,
With whispers full of cheer.

Children's laughter in the park,
Kites that soar in skies so clear,
Every moment leaves a mark,
A canvas bright with cheer.

Autumn leaves in amber glow,
Falling gently, year to year,
Nature's way to let us know,
There's beauty in each tear.

Smiles exchanged on city streets,
Warm embraces, hearts sincere,
In shared moments, joy retreats,
To whisper sweetly, cheer.

Nautical Joy

Beneath the sails, the dolphins play,
Across the waves, a sparkling day.
Gulls above in airy flight,
In joyous dance from morn till night.

The windy whispers through the ropes,
We chase the sun, fulfilling hopes.
Crashing foam in wild decree,
Nautical joy, so boundless, free.

In moon's embrace, the sea does gleam,
A sailor's heart, in dreams, redeemed.
Stars align, and wishes flow,
Across the currents' deepest glow.

Seascape Giggles

Shells and starfish on the shore,
Tales the ocean can't ignore.
Little crabs in sandy dance,
Seascape giggles in a trance.

Waves that tickle toes alike,
Seaweed threads in joyful hike.
Children splash in salty spree,
Laughter echoes, wild and free.

Sunlight sprinkles on the tide,
Boats and kites in summer glide.
Gentle breezes join the fun,
As giggles bloom beneath the sun.

Watery Whimsy

Mermaids hum a lullaby,
Underneath the azure sky.
Fish in colors bright, they spin,
Watery whimsy deep within.

Coral castles, vibrant hues,
Aqua ballet, gentle views.
Whales' soft whispers, secret tales,
In watery whimsy, magic sails.

Jellyfish like lanterns glow,
In the deep where dreams do flow.
Mystery in every glance,
A watery whimsy's subtle dance.

Marine Grace

Elegant beneath the blue,
Where the light and shadows strew.
Graceful dolphins, swift, concise,
Dancing in their liquid spice.

Turtle glides through kelp arrays,
Moving with a timeless grace.
Octopuses' silent reach,
In the depths, they softly preach.

Sunken ships, a story kept,
Silent vigils, oceans wept.
Marine grace in every glance,
Nature's art in fluid dance.

Aquatic Joy

Beneath the waves, the fish dance free,
Coral gardens, vibrant spree.
Sunlight pierces, shafts of gold,
Stories of the deep unfold.

Sea turtles glide in gentle grace,
Among the currents, find their place.
Dolphins leap and play so bright,
In this world of pure delight.

Anemones in colors bright,
Sway softly in the ocean light.
Whales sing songs, so deep and grand,
Echoes from a distant land.

Seagrass whispers, green and lush,
Crabs scuttle in a hurried rush.
Jellyfish like lanterns glow,
In the depths where currents flow.

Beneath the blue, a hidden bliss,
Nature's magic in abyss.
Every ripple, every tide,
Holds the ocean's secret pride.

Ocean's Secret

Beneath the waves, in shadows deep,
Secrets that the ocean keeps.
Whispered tales in currents stirred,
Mysteries without a word.

Hidden caverns, dark and cold,
Treasures of the ocean old.
Sunken ships in silent sleep,
Guard the secrets that they keep.

Pearls that shimmer, stories spun,
From the ocean's grasp, begun.
Creatures weave their silent lore,
Of the mysteries they adore.

Stars reflect on waves so still,
Mirroring the night's soft thrill.
Whispers of the deep do rise,
In the hush of moonlit skies.

Every splash and every wave,
Keep the secrets, ocean gave.
In the depths where light is scarce,
Lives a tale in every trance.

Sun-Kissed Waves

Golden rays on waves do rest,
Sunlight's kiss upon the crest.
Sparkling paths on water's face,
Nature's beauty in embrace.

Each wave dances with the sun,
In a rhythm, both are one.
Glittering jewels across the sea,
Whispering of eternity.

Warmth that flows from sky to deep,
Awakens life from slumber's sleep.
Every wave a gentle sigh,
Beneath the endless azure sky.

Seagulls cry and soar above,
In this haven, filled with love.
Sunsets paint the waves with fire,
A canvas that will never tire.

In the blush of evening light,
Waves reflect the sky's delight.
Sun-kissed dreams in every fold,
A tale in hues of blue and gold.

Parting Waves

Rise and fall, the ocean's song,
Echoes of where we belong.
Each wave's goodbye, a soft caress,
Memories in their recess.

Foam and spray on a journey fleet,
Mark the path where sea and sky meet.
As day departs, and light reflects,
Together we find what connects.

Ocean's Whisper

In the stillness, hear the call,
Ocean's whisper, faint and small.
Softly through the salty air,
Tales of wonder, free of care.

Gentle murmurs from the deep,
In the waves, secrets sleep.
Echoes of the ancient tales,
Carried on the midnight gales.

Foamy crests and rolling tides,
Hide where the ocean's spirit hides.
Every breeze a soft embrace,
From a distant, mystic place.

Whispers weave through shells and sand,
In a language of the land.
Secrets shared with those who hear,
Messages that seem so clear.

Listen close and you will find,
Ocean's voice both pure and kind.
Every wave and every sigh,
Whispers where the secrets lie.

Sea Sparkle

Waves like diamonds crest and fall,
Softly lit by twilight's call.
Silvery threads weave through the deep,
Secrets of the night they keep.

Moonbeams dance on rippling blue,
A cosmic waltz for me and you.
As tides embrace the sandy shore,
Daylight fades and dreams explore.

Seaside Whimsy

Whispers of the waves unfold,
Secrets carried, stories told.
Sand beneath a gentle sun,
Where dreams and tides as one.

Gulls above in circles weave,
Echoes of the sea they leave.
Footprints traced upon the shore,
Memories linger evermore.

Driftwood tales, the ocean's prose,
In salted breeze, a wish that grows.
Shells that sing of distant lands,
Treasures found by curious hands.

Starfish gleam in pools of blue,
Silent glories, nature's hue.
With every turn, the sea bestows,
A dance of life, where beauty flows.

Ocean's Twinkle

Stars reflected in the sea,
Every wave a galaxy.
Boundless sky and endless tides,
Meet where horizon gently glides.

Fish like comets dart below,
In the midnight's softest glow.
Silent mysteries unfold,
In twilight's grasp, tales retold.

Marine Mirage

Beneath the waves, a mystic sight,
Where sea and sky find quiet light.
Coral castles, vibrant bright,
In depths where day meets night.

Schools of silver, swift and sleek,
In silent ballet, secrets speak.
Caves where shadows softly creep,
A legacy that oceans keep.

Whales' songs in fathoms deep,
Echoes through the currents sweep.
Anemones in colors sprawled,
Nature's art in silence called.

Mirages in marine gleam,
Where reality blends with dream.
Swaying kelp in rhythmic trance,
A hidden world in watery dance.

Tidal Expressions

Tides roll in with whispered might,
Crafting worlds by day and night.
Patterns etched in shifting sands,
Ephemeral, by unseen hands.

Waves that crash with thundered voice,
In nature's symphony, rejoice.
Foam that kisses rocky strands,
A lover's touch on ancient lands.

Pools that gleam with life's display,
Where fleeting moments find their way.
Creatures small in tidal pools,
Tiny thrones for ocean's jewels.

Changing shores by moon's command,
Ebb and flow, a timeless band.
Tidal breaths in constant play,
Expressions of the ocean's sway.

Coastal Charm

Softly whispers morning light,
Over dunes' gentle height.
Seaglass gems with color bright,
Glimmer with the dawn's first sight.

Ships that sail on horizon's edge,
Bound for tales and secret pledge.
Fishermen with nets arrayed,
Harbor joys where hearts have stayed.

Boardwalk planks that creak and groan,
With stories of the sea they're shown.
Kites that flutter, high they roam,
Under skies, their boundless home.

Twilight falls with silvered grace,
Stars above in great embrace.
Coastal charm in every glance,
Where sea and shore in twilight dance.

Breezy Chuckle

Whispers ride on zephyrs light,
Tickling leaves in morning bright.
Laughter flits through fields of green,
Nature's joke, playfully seen.

Branches sway with fleeting mirth,
Echoes of the wind's rebirth.
Under skies where clouds collide,
Breath of life, in joy, abides.

Subaquatic Chuckle

Beneath the waves, where bubbles play,
A clownfish darts in bright array,
Charms crabs with jokes in coral maze,
Amidst the kelp, where moonbeams sway.

Octopuses twist their many arms,
In mirthful dance by seaweed farms,
While starfish giggle silently,
With currents whispering their alarms.

Jellyfish shiver, light a grin,
Around their tentacles, light's spin,
They sparkle jokes in silent streams,
In realms where laughter lies within.

A dolphin leaps, a pirouette,
Above the seafloor's pirouette,
Joy ripples through the waters clear,
Whale's bassy song, a duet.

So in the ocean's witty depth,
Life's mysteries in laughter kept,
Subaquatic chuckles flow,
Through liquid air, by Neptune's heft.

Ocean's Hush

In twilight tides, the ocean sleeps,
Waves murmur secrets in the deeps,
A lullaby to coral tombs,
Where life in silent cadence sweeps.

The moonlight waltzes on the crest,
A silver halo gently pressed,
Upon the sea's cerulean veil,
In tranquil rhythms, all unrest.

Soft whispers of anemones,
Caress the waters, calming seas,
In peace, the starfish take their dreams,
Amidst the currents, gentle breeze.

An ancient tale, the waves recite,
Of ships and sailors lost from sight,
Their echoes still within the hush,
By night, the sea's protective light.

So close your eyes, hear ocean's song,
A melody where dreams belong,
In hushed embrace by tidal grace,
Here, shadows rest and nights prolong.

Pearly Gleam

Within the shell, a secret glows,
A pearl of light, where mystery grows,
By ocean's heart, a tender find,
Of nature's art, where beauty shows.

Beneath the waves, it softly gleams,
A treasure forged in ocean's dreams,
Held tight in mollusk's safe embrace,
Amidst the sands and tidal streams.

Reflected stars in pearly view,
Eclipsed by night, yet shining true,
A cosmic dance within the sea,
In seeking hands, its beauty's due.

Diver's quest or seraph's tear,
A glistening orb, held dear,
In depths where silence reigns serene,
A silent song we long to hear.

Thus in the depth, the pearl remains,
With quiet strength through tempests' reigns,
A beacon soft in azure's glow,
Eternal light where darkened chains.

Seafaring Jest

On salty decks where sailors tread,
With maps and stars as guiding thread,
Adventure wraps in waves and gales,
    A jestful spirit overhead.

The albatross in wisdom steeped,
In gossip winds, old secrets keep,
While dolphins mock with playful arcs,
By hull and bow, their laughter leaped.

An old sea tale of mermaid's kiss,
Or Kraken's grip in tempest's hiss,
With hearty laughs and jests to spare,
The crew finds joy in ocean's bliss.

Night's lantern climbs the rigging ropes,
While sailors weave their dreams and hopes,
Each tale less truthful than the last,
Around the deck their laughter scopes.

In seafaring jest and merry mirth,
The briny deep is their rebirth,
For every wave their spirits crest,
Through endless seas they find their worth.

Seafloor Revelry

Beneath the waves in twilight's glow,
Secrets long hidden start to show.
Creatures dance with silent glee,
In the depths of the endless sea.

Coral castles light the way,
To where the ancient shipwrecks lay.
Whispers of the deep below,
Twisting tales that ebb and flow.

Seahorses waltz in graceful pair,
With plankton swirls that paint the air.
Eels peek from their caverned home,
In the ocean's catacomb.

Starfish glitter on the sands,
Like jewels in a pirate's hands.
The seafloor hums a gentle tune,
Beneath the light of the silver moon.

Sun-Drenched Grin

Golden rays kiss the earth,
Awakening joy and simple mirth.
Morning dew on petals bright,
Heralds the dawn's first light.

Children laugh and play outside,
With the sun as their guide.
Kites soar high in azure sky,
As the breezes gently fly.

Fields of daisies, sunlit dreams,
Glow beneath the daylight beams.
In every corner, the world does spin,
Underneath a sun-drenched grin.

Mountains stand with peaks aglow,
Bathed in sunlight's tender flow.
A tapestry of warmth and light,
From dawn 'til the fall of night.

Salty Chuckles

The sea breeze tells a thousand tales,
Of sailors braving storm and gales.
Laughter echoes from the shore,
Blended with the ocean's roar.

Old men gather, tales to spin,
With wrinkled faces and salty grins.
Memories of the youthful days,
In the sun's embrace, the salty haze.

Mermaids sing their ancient songs,
While waves do dance and winds belong.
Giggles burst from depths below,
Where coral reefs and fishes go.

Shells hold secrets, whispers light,
Of moonlit walks and starry night.
Salty chuckles fill the air,
With every tale that's told with care.

Rolling Waves

The rhythm of the ocean's sigh,
A lullaby beneath the sky.
Rolling waves in constant dance,
A timeless, endless, sweet romance.

Surfers ride the crests with pride,
On each thunderous, joyous tide.
The ocean's voice, a mighty roar,
With tales from every distant shore.

Sandcastles crafted by the hand,
Dissolve into the waiting sand.
In and out, the waves compete,
A never-ending, rhythmic beat.

Moonlight shimmers on the sea,
Casting spells of mystery.
Rolling waves, an ancient song,
Sung by the sea, where we belong.

Aqua Playfulness

In waters blue, where laughter swirls,
A dance of fish, the sea unfurls.
Fins and bubbles, joy cascade,
In liquid games, the light parade.

Sunbeams pierce through waves so bright,
Dolphins leap with pure delight.
Coral castles, colors blend,
In this play, all troubles mend.

Waves all giggle, crashing shore,
Children play and ask for more.
Shells and pebbles, in their hand,
Aqua joy at their command.

Tide pools shimmer, secrets hold,
In their depths, stories unfold.
Tiny crabs and starfish gleam,
In this playful water dream.

Moonlight dances on the crest,
Whispers to the sea at rest.
Dreams of blue in night's caress,
Aqua playfulness, no less.

Liquid Grin

Ripples chase the sinking sun,
Waves join in, the race begun.
Laughing gulls above the sea,
Whisper tales of where they've been.

Reflections play on surfaces,
Mirrors to the sun's caresses.
Wink of light, a liquid grin,
Kissed by the tide, the night begins.

Boats drift by, their shadows long,
Fishermen hum ancient songs.
Net and sea weave nightly kin,
Bound by water's playful spin.

Stars descend to water's edge,
Echoed in the ocean's pledge.
Each a smile, a twinkling kin,
In liquid's depth, a whispered grin.

Then the dawn, it blushes bright,
Moonlight yields to morning light.
Ocean grins, a new day in,
Eternal play, the liquid grin.

Harbor Humor

Boats align in gentle sway,
Colors bright, a break of day.
Masts and sails, a wooden grin,
Harbor wakes, let laughter in.

Fishermen and seagulls jest,
Morning bids the sea its best.
Ropes and nets, their stories spin,
In harbor's humor, life begins.

Barnacles cling, holding tight,
Shoreline glints in morning light.
Tales of ventures, far and near,
Sound of chuckles, sailing clear.

Lighthouse beams a winking eye,
Guiding ships where laughter lies.
Waves in concert, play their tune,
Harbor's humor, chilled to noon.

Twilight enters, sun descends,
Harbor's humor never ends.
In night's embrace, boats wait keen,
For dawn to wake their mirthful scene.

Seafoam Delight

Whispers rise from ocean's edge,
Seafoam kisses on the ledge.
Silver tides in morning light,
Dance upon the beach in flight.

Children chase the foamy trails,
Turn to giggles in their sails.
Crabs dart sideways in the sand,
Magic of the sea at hand.

Shells whisper secrets from the deep,
Seafoam stirs them from their sleep.
Each a story, soft and light,
In the wash of sea's delight.

Kites soar high in azure sky,
Surfboards ride the waves with sighs.
Frothy laughter, pure and bright,
Echoes in the seafoam's light.

Evening calls, the seagulls fly,
Sunset brushes sea and sky.
Whispers fade with fading light,
In the spell of seafoam's delight.

Seaside Laughter

The waves crash joyful at our feet,
In melodies, so wild, so sweet.
Laughter echoes with the breeze,
Moments treasured, hearts at ease.

Footprints linger in the sand,
Stories woven, hand in hand.
Salt-kissed whispers, secrets told,
New adventures yet unfold.

Gulls converse in airy flight,
Stars emerge in twilight's light.
Seaside laughter, pure and bright,
Memories that feel so right.

Cool waters and skies so blue,
Nature's canvas, ever true.
Sound of laughter fills the air,
With the ocean, joy we share.

With each tide, the day concludes,
Sunset paints in vivid hues.
Seaside laughter, love's embrace,
Endless joys in this sacred place.

Beneath the Waves

Submerged in silence, cool and deep,
Worlds of wonder, secrets keep.
Beings drift in fluid grace,
Liquid realms, a hidden place.

Coral forests, colors bright,
In this realm, no day or night.
Gliding shadows, soft embrace,
Mysteries in every trace.

Whales' low songs traverse the sea,
Echo through eternity.
Dawns are distant, lights that gleam,
Beneath the waves, a timeless dream.

Tides of life in currents danced,
Ebb and flow, an ancient trance.
Beneath the waves, a life unfolds,
Tales unnumbered, yet untold.

Journeyed depths, our spirits freed,
In the blue, our souls are freed.
Beneath the waves, where dreams reside,
We find our peace, the ocean's pride.

Ephemeral Waters

Rivers whisper through the land,
Every curve a gentle hand.
Fleeting moments, currents swift,
In their dance, our spirits lift.

Mountains' tears transform to streams,
Echoing our hopes and dreams.
Waters flowing, time's caress,
In their passage, we find rest.

Every droplet, history,
Tiny tales of mystery.
Ephemeral as morning dew,
Carrying life, renews anew.

Daylight gleams on placid lakes,
Reflections of the dawn it takes.
Ripples spread, a brief ballet,
Touching shores, they float away.

Silent pools and rushing falls,
Nature's answer to our calls.
Ephemeral waters, journeys brief,
In their paths, we find relief.

Sunlit Ocean

Golden rays caress the sea,
Light and water, eternally.
Sunlit ocean, sparkling bright,
Reveling in pure delight.

Crystalline by dawn's embrace,
Endless blue, a tranquil place.
Dancing lights on crests so fine,
Nature's art in grand design.

Boats that drift on glassy bays,
Charting paths through golden haze.
Sunlit waters, vast and wide,
Where horizon and dreams collide.

Holding worlds 'neath surface sheen,
Silent, deep, and so serene.
Sunlit ocean, whisper clear,
In its arms, we disappear.

Endless sky and endless sea,
Bound together, wild and free.
Sunlit ocean, heart's release,
In its glow, we find our peace.

Laughing Tides

Waves frolic in gleeful might,
Under the pale moon's light,
Sandy shores echo their cheer,
Contours of joy ever near.

Foamy crests dance with zeal,
Secrets in their folds conceal,
Mirthful tides in endless spree,
Whispers of the deep sea.

With each surge, a story told,
By shores both young and old,
Bubbles burst with sweet delight,
In the symphony of night.

Ebb and flow, a playful chase,
Nature's grin, a soft embrace,
In the realm where waters play,
Tides of laughter sway.

Silence breaks with each wave's kiss,
Bringer of serene bliss,
In laughing tides' gentle grip,
Oceans share their sweet quip.

Ocean's Gleam

Golden rays on water's crest,
Silent ripples at sun's request,
Shimmering hues in twilight's beam,
Nature's smile in ocean's gleam.

Dance of light on azure spread,
Fleeting moments softly tread,
Essence of the daybreak's dream,
Captured in the ocean's gleam.

Dolphins leap in joyous play,
In the glow of breaking day,
Mirrored skies in water's theme,
Underneath the ocean's gleam.

Moon and stars in night's embrace,
Glimmers on the surface trace,
Celestial waltz in silver seam,
Mesmerized by ocean's gleam.

Eternity in every glance,
Waves in an endless dance,
Magic of the sun's esteem,
Breathes within the ocean's gleam.

Salty Guffaw

Seagull's cry, a jolly jest,
Waves joining, never rest,
Salt and breeze in playful draw,
Nature laughs in salty guffaw.

Pebbles tickle, sand in play,
With the rolling surf of day,
Laughing seas around the bay,
Join the salty guffaw's sway.

Whales breach with grand delight,
In the ocean's soft twilight,
Echoes of their joy withdraw,
Lost within the salty guffaw.

Shells that sing with every swoon,
By the light of sun and moon,
Secrets whispered to shore's paw,
In rhythms of the salty guffaw.

Children's laughter, breezy tunes,
Till the rise of silver moons,
Creases in the day's tableau,
Shaped by every salty guffaw.

Ripples of Mirth

With a splash of joyous cheer,
Ripples spread both far and near,
Echoes of their hearty birth,
In the ripples of sweet mirth.

Pebble's plunge in water's grace,
Sends a ripple to embrace,
Each one carries joy's true worth,
Born of gentle ripples of mirth.

Sunlight's dance on liquid stage,
Tales of joy on every page,
Waves recall their ancient birth,
Weaving tales in ripples of mirth.

Every crest a smiling face,
In the ocean's warm embrace,
Laughter in the water's girth,
Lives within the ripples of mirth.

Nature's heart in rhythmic beat,
Laughter's touch in waves discreet,
Infinite their joy and girth,
Intertwined in ripples of mirth.

Ocean's Echo

Waves crash upon the distant shore,
With tales of lands unknown before.
The salty spray, the seagulls' cry,
Beneath the vast and endless sky.

The sun sinks low, a fiery blaze,
Reflecting dreams of bygone days.
Shells whisper secrets to the sand,
As tides caress the sleeping land.

Moonlight dances on water's crest,
Inviting souls to come and rest.
In ocean's depths, where silence reigns,
Lies heartbeats of ancient refrains.

Silent Waters

A mirror calm, the lake lies still,
Reflecting woods and distant hill.
In dawn's first light, the world seems new,
A canvas brushed with morning dew.

The ripples tell of fleeting time,
Eternal peace, a silent rhyme.
Through willow's grace, a gentle sigh,
A melody of lullabies.

Silent waters hold dreams tight,
Beneath the stars' celestial light.
With whispers soft, through winds that sway,
Night fades in the arms of day.

Whispers of the Deep

In depths where darkness meets the light,
Lie secrets hidden from our sight.
The oceans whisper tales below,
Of worlds we may yet never know.

Through coral forests, fish dart by,
In dances silent as they fly.
Anemones with colors bright,
Sing songs of deep and endless night.

Beneath the waves, in caverns grand,
Lie mysteries we understand.
Not with our eyes, but with our dreams,
In watery realms where no one beams.

Coastal Serenade

Soft melodies from waves that play,
Along the shore at break of day.
The soft, sweet hum of tranquil seas,
Sings through the whispers of the breeze.

Palm trees sway in rhythmic dance,
To tunes of ancient, sung romance.
Sand beneath our feet feels warm,
In nature's raw, untroubled form.

From dusk till dawn, the sea endures,
A symphony of loves so pure.
A coastal serenade, refined,
Echoes through the heart and mind.

Surf's Humor

The waves seem to chuckle, a frothy parade,
As surfers dance on this liquid arcade.
Saltwater whispers, a jesting delight,
Under the sun's warm, gleaming spotlight.

Seagulls are laughing, swooping in glee,
Echoes of joy, wild and free.
Sand crabs giggle, digging below,
The shore's subtle humor, a soft undertow.

Boards glide like mirth over ocean's grin,
Riders in sync with the playful spin.
Splashes of fun in a tidal pun,
Where humor and ocean meld into one.

A tumble, a stumble, salty embrace,
Waves tease with their watery grace.
Each wipeout met with a hearty cheer,
Laughing aloud, conquering fear.

Sunset falls, the laughter lingers,
Echoes carried on breeze fingers.
Surf's humorous waltz, day's final bow,
Leaving joy for the morrow's surf to endow.

Playful Depths

Beneath the surface, a world to explore,
In quiet whispers where mysteries soar.
Fishes dart with games unplanned,
In depths where play and stillness stand.

Coral castles, vibrant and bright,
Hosts to a maze of playful delight.
Anemones dance in the sea's soft breath,
A ballet beneath, defying death.

Turtles drift in a languid race,
Gliding through their aqueous space.
In shadows and sunlight, they twist and turn,
A lesson of joy in freedom we learn.

Octopus trickster in hide-and-seek,
Cleverly blending, a cunning mystique.
Laughing underwater, a silent cheer,
Ingenious games in the ocean sphere.

Playful depths, a secretive fun,
Under moon's glow or midday sun.
A realm of whimsy below the waves,
Where the sea's deepest laughter saves.

Floating Euphoria

Floating on waves, lost in a dream,
Sun's gentle kiss, a radiant beam.
Euphoria whispers in watery song,
A liquid embrace, where hearts belong.

Clouds drift by in a serene ballet,
The sea's tender lullaby on display.
Weightless we move in a dance so free,
Echoes of bliss in the vast blue sea.

Eyes closed, we drift, on nature's crest,
In buoyant arms, we find our rest.
Joy flows as time loses its claim,
Letting go in euphoria's name.

Salt on our lips, a taste of the divine,
Merging with the rhythm of Neptune's line.
Each wave a symphony, each swell a kiss,
Floating away in euphoric bliss.

Boundless and free, we glide and sway,
In harmony's touch, we choose to stay.
Floating euphoria, serene and bright,
In the sea's embrace, we take flight.

Hidden Beneath

Secrets lie in the ocean deep,
Where light is scarce, and shadows creep.
Hidden beneath the surface bold,
Mysteries wait in the silent cold.

Fathoms below, in a sacred shroud,
Creatures live, both fierce and proud.
Whispers of old in the dark abyss,
A history etched in the ocean's kiss.

Lost treasures rest in watery graves,
Ancient ships and unmarked caves.
Echoes of legends, tales unsung,
Buried where the seaweed's hung.

Silent sentinels of the ocean floor,
Guardians of secrets behind a door.
Life moves in the muted light,
Hidden wonders in the endless night.

Hidden beneath, the world unknown,
In the ocean's depths, seeds are sown.
Of life and mystery, dark and bright,
In the silent deep, stars ignite.

Hidden Humor

Laughter echoes in the night,
Whispers dance on lips so light,
Jokes untold, in shadows bloom,
Merry secrets in the gloom.

Eyes that sparkle, mischief's glow,
Wit as swift as rivers flow,
In the quiet, humor weaves,
Subtle smiles like rustling leaves.

Chuckle softly, hearts entwine,
Humor hidden, yet divine,
Unseen jesters play their part,
Tickling thoughts, a gentle art.

Silent giggles, softly shared,
Humor's magic, freely aired,
In the hush, a comic twist,
Lingers like a fleeting mist.

Grins that gleam in muted light,
Hidden humor in the night,
Kindred spirits, jest unseen,
Quiet mirth, a gentle sheen.

Sandy Secrets

Beneath the dunes, where shadows creep,
Whispers of the sands do keep,
Secrets ancient, buried deep,
Silent tales in endless sleep.

Footprints lost in golden waves,
Echoes where the ocean paves,
Every grain a hidden trove,
Time and tide where secrets rove.

Whispers of the oceans' sigh,
Sandy secrets, passing by,
On the shore where heartbeats blend,
Stories whispered to the wind.

Moonlit nights and starry skies,
Underneath, the essence lies,
In the grains that slip and play,
Sandy secrets, night and day.

Waves of time and tales to tell,
In the dunes where whispers swell,
Sandy secrets, softly shared,
Memories in silence spared.

Salt-Kissed Jest

Where the sea breeze plays and sings,
Laughter on the salt wind clings,
Jests that rise from ocean's crest,
Salt-kissed humor at its best.

Mermaids' chuckles, sailors' glee,
Jests that sail the endless sea,
Crashing waves and playful tease,
Echoes of their ocean ease.

In the froth, the jesters hide,
Salt-kissed mirth, a joyous ride,
Seagulls' cries and dolphins' leap,
Laughing waves that never sleep.

Salted air and humor bright,
Glistening beneath the light,
A funny tale, a breezy jest,
Ocean's laughter, never rest.

Waves that whisper jokes untold,
Salt-kissed jest that never old,
By the shore or out at sea,
Humor dances, wild and free.

Joyful Current

In the river's merry flow,
Joyful currents come and go,
Laughing eddies, playful swirl,
Nature's dance, a joyous whirl.

Fish that leap in sunlit streams,
Chasing sunlight, casting gleams,
Currents whisper, secrets laugh,
Nature's song on water's staff.

Ripples giggle, waves delight,
Joyful current, crystal bright,
Flowing down with gentle grace,
Smiles of water, sweet embrace.

Light and shadow interlace,
In the current's joyous race,
Laughter blends with bubbling sound,
Nature's happiness abounds.

By the banks where flowers sway,
Joyful currents find their way,
In each ripple, laughter flows,
Joy in every breeze that blows.

Mystery of the Tides

In moonlit whispers, waves unfold,
Their secrets told, yet still concealed.
With ebb and flow, mysteries told,
In tides, the ocean's heart revealed.

Shadows dance on sandy shores,
Drawing near, then pulling back.
A cryptic waltz, forever more,
In nature's undulating track.

Stars above in midnight sky,
Mirror waters deep and wide.
Silent questions riding high,
Answered only by the tide.

The ancient pull of lunar force,
Guiding waters far and near.
Nature's law, an endless course,
Tides, the earth and moon endear.

Whispers of the ocean's lore,
In every wave, the truth resides.
The sea's vast heart forevermore,
The mystery of its endless tides.

Seaside Gleam

Golden rays on morning sand,
A gentle breeze through dunes so grand.
The ocean's kiss, a morning brine,
Reflecting light, a gleaming find.

Shells that sparkle in the sun,
Waves that dance, their race begun.
Footprints wash with each new wave,
Memories in the tide engraved.

The lighthouse stands with solemn grace,
Guiding ships to a safe embrace.
In the twilight, beams of light,
Pierce the veil of coming night.

Children's laughter, joyous sounds,
Echo through the seaside grounds.
Building castles made of dreams,
In sync with nature's gentle streams.

As dusk descends upon the shore,
The gleam of day does fade once more.
Yet in the night, stars take the stage,
A cosmic show, forever sage.

Beneath the Blue

Below the surface, life at play,
A hidden world where creatures sway.
Coral gardens, colors bright,
In endless dance, a pure delight.

Fish with scales of shimmering hue,
Dart through waters, swift and true.
In currents warm, they glide and weave,
A ballet only sea can conceive.

Seagrass meadows, gently sweep,
In ocean's arms, they softly leap.
Crabs in caverns, starfish too,
In this world beneath the blue.

Octopus with minds so keen,
Masters of disguise unseen.
A tapestry of life unfolds,
In depths where secret tales are told.

From reef to reef, the rhythms flow,
In silent whispers, undertow.
Beneath the blue, the heart does beat,
In ocean's pulse, life's symphony complete.

Printed in the USA
CPSIA information can be obtained
at www.ICGtesting.com
CBHW071845180824
13303CB00040B/1000